Crocodiles Can't Cli

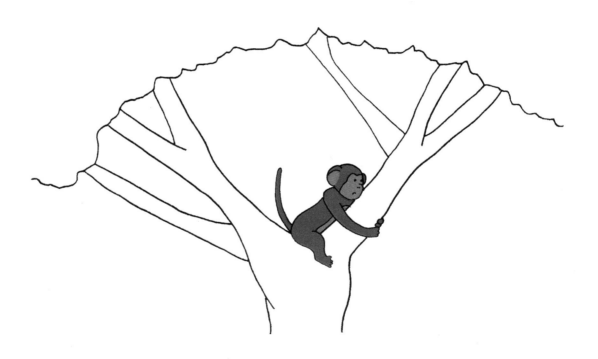

Once there was a **c**ute little monkey called Lu**c**a.

Luca liked to **kick** his so**cc**er ball around by the river bank.

Kick kick kick, all day long.

One day **K**evin the Cro**c**odile snu**ck** up the river
and saw Lu**c**a **kick**ing his ball around.
He wanted to **c**atch Lu**c**a!

Lu**c**a **c**ould see **K**evin **c**oming to **c**atch him, so he quickly **c**apered away.

Lu**c**a hid behind a sa**ck** of **c**arrots
but **K**evin's teeth **c**ut right through

-k-k-k-k-k-k-k-k-k-k-k-k-k-k-

Lu**c**a snu**ck** behind a **c**art of **c**orn,
but **K**evin's teeth **c**ut right through

-k-k-k-k-k-k-k-k-k-k-k-k-k-k-k-

Lu**c**a crouched behind a bu**ck**et of pi**ck**les,
but **K**evin's teeth **c**ut right through

-k-k-k-k-k-k-k-k-k-k-k-k-k-k-k-k-

Lu**c**a hid behind a giant ro**ck**
but **K**evin's teeth **c**ut right through

-k-k-k-k-k-k-k-k-k-k-k-k-k-k-k-k-k-

So Lu**c**a did the last thing he **c**ould think of.
He climbed up high in the tallest and
thi**ck**est tree he **c**ould find.

Kevin tried as hard as he **c**ould,
but his teeth **c**ould not **c**ut
through the thi**ck** trunk!

Finally, Lu**c**a was safe tucked up high in the branches — be**c**ause cro**c**odiles **c**an't climb trees!